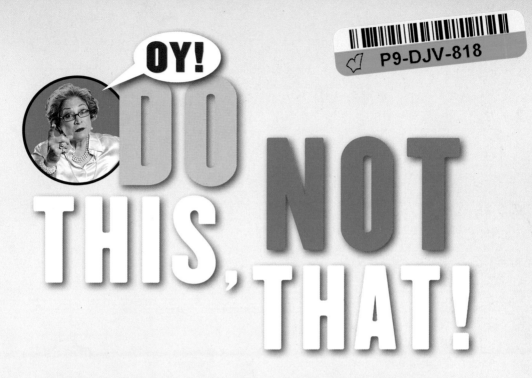

OY!

DO THIS, NOT THAT!

100 SIMPLE SWAPS that Can Save Your Life, Your Money,
or Your Mother from a Heart Attack, **God Forbid!**

by **ELLIS WEINER**

RUNNING PRESS
PHILADELPHIA · LONDON

◇◇◇◇◇◇◇◇◇◇◇◇◇◇◇◇◇

9 8 7 6 5 4 3 2 1
Digit on the right indicates the number of this printing

Library of Congress Control Number: 2009930849

ISBN 978-0-7624-3883-9

Cover: (top left) photo by J. Nichole Smith; (top right) ©Thinkstock, LLC;
(bottom left) ©iStockphoto.com/dolgikh

Design: Kasey Free and Todd Bates
Editorial: Kjersti Egerdahl
Photo Research: Jessica Eskelsen
Production Coordination: Tom Miller

Oy! Do This, Not That is produced by becker&mayer!, Bellevue, Washington
www.beckermayer.com

Running Press Book Publishers
2300 Chestnut Street
Philadelphia, PA 19103-4371

Visit us on the web!
www.runningpress.com

Contents

Introduction 4

All Your Favorite Advice 6

Mother Decoder 64

Holidays and Special Occasions 66

Take This, Not That! 78

Do This, Not That—for the Children! 80

Glossary 92

Index 94

Image Credits 96

Introduction ⟨∞∞∞∞∞∞∞∞∞∞∞∞∞∞∞∞∞∞∞∞⟩

THE TOP TEN SWAPS TO MAKE YOUR MOTHER DIE HAPPY

For Men

1. **DO THIS:** Become a professional—a doctor, lawyer, CPA, MBA.
   NOT THAT: Do something so-called "creative" for a living.

2. **DO THIS:** Get married.
   NOT THAT: Keep stalling. I'm not getting any younger and I'd like to be around for the wedding.

3. **DO THIS:** Have children.
   NOT THAT: Deny me grandchildren because of your fancy-schmancy "lifestyle."

4. **DO THIS:** Get exercise and see many doctors often.
   NOT THAT: Jump out of airplanes or climb Mount Everest or become some kind of alcoholic or, God forbid, drug addict.

5. **DO THIS:** Call me at least once a week and visit often.
   NOT THAT: Start with the computer and the e-mails, like I don't have enough machinery in the house.

For Women

1. **DO THIS:** Get married. Try that JDate on the computer. That's how Lil Horowitz's daughter met that Jeffrey.
   NOT THAT: Be "independent" or let yourself become an old maid.

2. **DO THIS:** Have children. Two or three.
   NOT THAT: Be self-centered or lazy and have none, or be one of those *meshuge frummies* with six or seven.

3. **DO THIS:** Find some kind of sensible career until you get married.
   NOT THAT: Do something dangerous or irresponsible or pointless, like become a folksinger or a writer.

4. **DO THIS:** Take care of your children's health first, your husband's health second, and your own health (and hair) third.
   NOT THAT: Act like the Queen of Sheba or be all vain like a fashion plate.

5. **DO THIS:** Call me every day and come visit with your children and husband often.
   NOT THAT: Go live in Hotzeplotz somewhere far away, especially since your father and I are lonely now that the Cohens have moved to Boca.

All Your Favorite Advice

◇◇◇◇◇◇◇◇◇◇◇◇◇◇◇

Did You Know, Mr. Big Shot?

Good posture shows everyone that you have lovely parents who care about how their child appears. And don't tell me it doesn't matter how you look because that's "not the real you or your true inner self." Nobody cares about the real you except your parents and your sister.

Oy Vey!

Remember my Aunt Rose? With the hump back? She didn't stand up straight either. But look at how nice that Mandy Patinkin stands.

Do This

Stand up straight!

Put your shoulders back and hold your head up like a person.

Look other people in the eye!

Not That!

Slouch like a *putz*.

Bad posture is the number one cause of people thinking you're a hoodlum.

Slump like a *shmendrik* on the sofa.

PLEASURE? GUILTY!

Don't tell me it's natural to stand like that. The heck with "natural." What if it was natural to jump off a cliff!? It's just your way of trying to torment me. Plus what if your spine freezes?

HIDDEN DANGER

When you slouch around like that, people think, "*Gevalt*, what poor posture. I'm not hiring *her* for any good-paying job."

At a good college you not only become an educated individual, but you meet people who will be important contacts later in life. They will become highly influential persons who can give you "a leg up" in the career of your choice. So don't laugh.

And by the way, "good" does not mean running around and getting inebriated at those fraternity houses you frequent. It means acquiring the professional excellence from studying and working hard to be a prominent, capable individual in your chosen field of study, which is medicine.

Do This

Go to a good college.

And "good" does not mean "fun." It means Ivy League or maybe Stanford.

Socialize with an appropriate, nice element.

Not That!

"Take a year off" like some kind of bum.

You can't just become studious again all of a sudden after a year.

Volunteer to teach poor Africans how to use computers.

Don't You Know?

Why do you think there are all those TV shows about doctors and lawyers? Because those people are admired in society. When you're an MD or a dentist or a lawyer or an MBA executive or a whatchamacallit, CPA, you work for yourself and you can't be fired.

HIDDEN DANGER

A therapist with a PhD is not the same as a psychiatrist with an MD. But who wants to talk to crazy people all day? The heck with both of them. Be a radiologist.

Do This

Become a professional.

You make a nice living and you're your own boss.

Specialize in whatever is the coming thing.

Not That!

Become a so-called "creative" type or "artist."

LITTLE TRICK

You think you're a creative person? Fine. If you're a doctor or a lawyer, you can write books like that John Grisham or TV shows or whatever. Because you'll know what you're talking about. Then, when you can't make a success of it, at least you'll have something to fall back on.

People in show business become alcoholics and artists become drug addicts. Who needs it?

Oy Vey!

A PhD in the humanities is, they call you "doctor" but you're really a teacher. It's a respectable profession but look at those people, the problems they have with the tenure and so forth.

Turn into a religious nut.

Studies in *People* magazine in the dentist's office show that married people live longer and are happier, believe it or not. Why? Because the human person needs a companion. Your father was twenty-three when we got married and aside from the spastic colon and the bypass he's had a perfectly wonderful life. Plus, of course, when you get married you can have the fulfillment of children, which is such a main part of the human drama. And then grandchildren, *keynahore*.

Do This

Get married.

Fall in love with someone nice.

Harriet's daughter just got her master's degree. Who cares in what? She's a lovely girl.

Not That!

"Date"!

Who "dates"? Teenagers "date."

Sleep around and get diseases.

PLEASURE? GUILTY!

What are you, a playboy? Enough already with the "dating." Your cousin Nathan married that lovely Shelley and now my sister has a beautiful grandson, what's his name— Connor . . . or Cobalt . . . Argyle—I don't know, one of these trendy *goyishe* names they like these days.

LITTLE TRICK

That speed dating thing on 60 Minutes *or whatever—give it a try. You're very busy, I understand that. So is the wife you'll marry, if she's not a schlump. And no, it's not dating. It's shopping. Look, who cares how you meet people? You go out, you go to bed, you fall in love, boom, it's done.*

Believe me, it's not for religious reasons. I'm not saying you have to be Jewish-Jewish and have an observant household, Orthodox, Conservative, any of that. You want to be *frum*, you want to eat lobster, that's your business. Look, marry whoever you want, as long as he shares your upbringing and culture and history.

You know the expression, it's just as easy to fall in love with a rich man as a poor man? Well it's even easier to fall in love with a nice rich Jewish boy!

Do This

Marry a nice Jewish boy.

Jews make good husbands. Ask anyone.

Make sure he's from a nice family.

Not That!

Marry some *sheygets*.

Forget you. Think of the children.

Fool around with different religions or races.

Yes, very funny, a Jewish mother says marry a doctor. But have you ever asked yourself why, Miss College-Educated Feminist? I'll tell you why. Because people will always get sick. It is a fact of life. A doctor will always find employment.

So start looking for one. But not from a clinic. An important one. Like a gastroenterologist or an invasive neurological surgeon. They have the private practice and are highly respected. And don't tell me you don't know how you'll find one who's interested, because of course you will, because look at you.

Do This

Marry a doctor!

Don't laugh. They're good providers.

Find a specialist. Not a GP.

Not That!

Marry a teacher or a policeman or etcetera.

They are fine people, but not as a husband.

Fool around with plumbers and mechanics.

PLEASURE? GUILTY!

Love is great, but life is full of economic realities after love cools off. A doctor is the one person everybody needs. Well, maybe a lawyer. But most of them, in my experience, they hate their job and it drives them crazy.

LITTLE TRICK

If you are dating a man who is not a doctor (such as, for example, a football player or a musician), ask yourself, "Wouldn't this be better if he were a doctor?" And then, since the answer will be "yes," stop dating him and look for a real doctor.

You are the man. That means the main provider, who has to work regardless. She is the mother of your children. So she is in charge of the house. Period.

I know she works and has a career and so forth, but who is going to breast-feed the baby? You? But as long as she's home, you want someone who knows how to cook and make a nice environ-ment. Of course hire a girl to clean once a week, the point is: there is a reason for tradition.

Do This

Marry a girl who's a good homemaker.

After you work hard all day, you are entitled to some comfort.

If she can't cook, make her learn.

Not That!

Marry a girl you have to serve like the Queen of Sheba.

2

Number of credit cards I had when you were growing up. An American Express for every-day and the Visa for emergencies because of the finance charge.

No one likes a vain girl who has to be waited on hand and foot.

HIDDEN DANGER

Don't fall for that "I'm worth it" business. These entitled girls act like shopping is an art form. They look great—and you end up in the poorhouse.

End up with a wife who constantly splurges.

Did You by Any Chance Know?

A wedding isn't really for you. It's like a funeral. It's for everybody else. I'll give you a list of our friends we want you to invite. They all remember when you were a little boy and they want to *kvell*. Of course assuming you have made a proper choice of a wife from a civilized family. Not like that what's-her-name you dated in college. Otherwise everyone stands around and looks at each other and thinks, "*Oy*— this is the mother of his children? If she even lets him have any?"

Do This

Have a lovely wedding with a rabbi, a reception, and a dinner.

So what if it's expensive. You only do it once.

Make sure the band plays real music.

Not That!

Get married at City Hall— or, worse, elope.

You think you're avoiding a lot of unnecessary to-do and expense, but people ask themselves: what are they hiding? Are they ashamed or embarrassed? Okay, you say you don't care what people think. But yes you do. Everybody does.

LITTLE TRICK

Tell your fiancée to tell her parents that the two of you are thinking about skipping the wedding. They'll volunteer to handle the whole thing. All you have to do is show up in a nice suit. Here, I'll give you a check for it, as a wedding present.

I don't understand such things. Why bother?

Have a quiet, private ceremony. *Feh*.

As I'm Sure You Know

You want to live among people who have some *tam*. You do so know what it means, I use it all the time. *Tam*. It means . . . you know . . . *tam*. Flavor! Personality! People with *tam* are intelligent people who are involved in the world. Plus the museums and restaurants. The offerings of a proper society.

And especially for the children. This is what cities are for. Everyone is talking and doing and caring about things. The suburbs are fine. Although a lot of them aren't what they used to be, so be careful.

Do This

Live in or at least near a civilized city.

Which means near me, so I can see my grandchildren.

Live nicely and not in a dump.

Not That!

Run off to the rural boondocks or a foreign country or some island.

Outside the cities America is all *goyim* and rednecks.

LITTLE TRICK

I'm not saying you have to live surrounded by Jews. But find a place with a nice Jewish community. That's how you know you'll be in the presence of an adequate level of civilization. The non-Jews will also be nice, which I have nothing against, believe me.

End up in one of the rectangular states.

I don't understand this "natural child-birth" craze, with the breathing and the pain. To what end? What purpose is served by all this suffering and screaming? All it does is frighten the baby. And who cares about "natural"? Polio is natural, too! You want the baby should get that, God forbid?

Of course I'm not as "with it" as you, but in my opinion we have hospitals and anesthetics for a reason. So use them. Take it from me, the baby will give you enough things to scream about soon enough.

Do This

Have your babies in a proper hospital with an obstetrician and anesthetics.

There is no need to look for ways to suffer, believe me.

Use real MD's.

Not That!

Have one of those *farkakte* New Age births, at home, in the bathtub.

Who does this? Who willingly exposes their newborn infant to possibly drowning? And why? So the baby has a few more seconds to pretend it hasn't been born? Swimming around like it's still inside the mother?

And don't even talk to me about the sofa.

5

The minimum number of qualified professionals who should be there when your baby is born.

Pretend you're a cavewoman and have a midwife.

Circumcising the male child is the oldest Jewish tradition there is. Period. Five thousand years we've been doing this without a problem. Now suddenly there's some crazy movement to say it's no good? Ridiculous.

And unhealthy! It is a matter of medical cleanliness and basic hygiene to have that area un-covered-up so it can't harbor any impurities.

If you don't want to have a *bris*, fine. I can see how a modern person might think that's too primitive. Then have them do it in the hospital under those conditions.

Do This

Make sure your sons are circumcised.

It's traditional *because* it's healthy.

Ask if you need me to find a *mohel*.

Not That!

Let them go around with a *goyishe* pecker.

A Jewish boy's identity starts with his not having a foreskin.

Oy Vey!

Ask yourself how your son will feel when he is at camp or the country club, and he takes off his bathing suit and sees that his penis is different from all the other penises around him.

HIDDEN DANGER

Don't tell me you're letting it be his "choice" once he's grown up. Some choice. Who would want to be Jewish if it meant you had to choose this kind of thing? That's why we do it when they're babies!

As Everybody Knows

I never had an opportunity to learn a musical instrument. Neither did your father. So who knows what kind of aptitude we could have had. But you kids did and your children should, too.

The piano is the basic thing. The violin, frankly, that sad, tragic Russian-Jewish-type shtetl music reminds me of my grandparents and I want to kill myself, I get so depressed. So make them play happy music.

Ballet is very lovely for the girls. I know they'll end up in *The Nutcracker* over Christmas, but what can you do.

Do This

Make sure the kids take piano lessons.

Or the girls can take ballet.

And make sure they practice.

Not That!

Let them learn anything that makes that rock and roll-type noise.

It's your house. They can make noise when they move out.

Pay for tap dancing or other *meshugas*.

Look, what goes on in the bedroom between you and your spouse is entirely your affair, so let me tell you something: too much is just as bad as not enough.

We used to know a couple, never mind who, it's all they did. They talked about it and made jokes about it and it made everyone very uncomfortable. And of course I felt terrible, since it made your father think he was missing something.

So do yourself a favor and try to obtain a balance. Of normal activity.

Do This

Have a normal sex life.

This is none of my business, but still.

Once you're married, be *married*.

32

Not That!

Be, God forbid, a "swinger," with the key parties and Plato's Treat.

This trading and swapping— it's for the *goyim*. Even the black people don't do that.

"Experiment" with your "lifestyle" like those sex communists in Oregon.

Permit Me to Inform You So You Know

A healthy person is a person who eats in a healthy manner and has some meat on her bones. A woman should look like a woman and not a boy or a stick. These models, I don't know why you think they're so perfect, they look like they wandered out of the camps in nice clothes. Besides, they make themselves skinny professionally, for the camera. Is someone paying you to take your picture for a magazine? Where you have to be skinny in person so you look nice in the picture?

Do This

Eat! You're too skinny.

Why does everyone have to look like a fashion model?

Don't be afraid of dessert. Live a little!

Not That!

Oy, not that much!

Take care of your figure while you're still young enough to have one.

Let yourself go—and so soon.

Oy Vey!

All that *fressing*—it's not healthy. All it takes is, gain one pound a year. One pound a year, and before you know it you look like your father's Aunt Miriam. Fat.

There are a million diets—to lose weight, to gain weight, to have more energy . . . if you ask me, it's all baloney. That Atkins—my sister was on it. She told me what it does, I couldn't believe it. It keeps your body in some kind of artificial state! Who lives this way?

PLEASURE? GUILTY!

Everybody likes a treat. But don't stuff yourself with ice cream just because you had a bad day at work, or some *schmuck* doesn't call you back, or whatever. Eat because you're happy. If you're sad, have a drink.

Do This

Eat like a *person*.

A diet of all-this or all-that . . . I don't believe in it.

If you're gaining weight, just eat *less*.

Not That!

Become a vegetarian—or, God forbid, a vegan. Kosher is up to you.

Oy Vey!

This not eating meat because it's mean to the animals—I don't understand this. Then don't wear leather! Then don't swat mosquitoes! We are all animals and we eat one another. As for this vegan business— no dairy? No eggs? Completely *tsedrayt*.

Mankind is an eater of meat. Not of twigs and crazy grasses.

LITTLE TRICK

If you feel bad for the animals but you still want to eat like a human being, you can try keeping kosher. There's something they do involved with being humane to the chickens.

Get crazy with organic, which is a racket.

These are healthy, popular sports that don't involve any banging into people or falling down. With tennis, all right, you can pull something. So be careful and wear a sweater.

But the main thing is, half the business in the world is conducted on the golf course. Everybody plays golf. If you're prepared to say yes if someone invites you to play, then you can close the deal or impress the boss or whatever the situation may be.

With tennis you can hobnob with the upper crust, which wouldn't kill you either.

Do This

Learn to play golf and tennis and other normal sports.

Not just for fun, but for the social benefits.

Join a country club and take advantage.

Not That!

Tie rubber bands to your legs and jump off bridges and cliffs.

Why do you have to almost die to have recreation?

Fool around with boxing, surfing, or gliders.

Oy Vey!

No one who ever got injured sky-diving or doing one of those other crazy sports, got up in the morning thinking, "I think I'll break my neck today." Doesn't that tell you something?

PLEASURE? GUILTY!

Those people who jump out of airplanes for "kicks" and whatnot—does it ever occur to them that their children need them? Especially if they don't have children yet? Who therefore cannot ever be born if "the unthinkable" happens?

Everybody loves the beach. The ocean is magnificent. The sand is fun for the children. The sea breezes are pleasant and refreshing. You expose yourself to the sun to get hot, and then cool off in the water, so every-thing evens out.

Of course you have to be careful people don't steal your valuables when your back is turned in the water. Or that time your father got hit in the head with a Frisbee. And those people flying kites, they'll run right over you, they don't care.

Do This

Take your family to the beach.

Enjoy the sun and the sand and the surf and turf.

Stand by the ocean and *breathe*, because the air is healthy.

Not That!

Forget to wear sunblock, long sleeves, hats, sandals, socks, and maybe pants.

The sun is no joke and the water is an *ocean*.

Eat any shellfish. By now it's poison.

HIDDEN DANGER

Bring insect repellent and sunglasses so you don't go blind. Between the hours of ten AM and two PM be sure you are completely clothed and under a blanket.

PLEASURE? GUILTY!

Do not go into the water for at least ninety minutes after eating anything, and never go into the water above your ankles. Jumping around in the waves is for hoodlums. Always watch the lifeguards. Bring extra water, a first aid kit, and a cell phone. Enjoy!

We naturally assume that everyone lives as we do, and then you travel to Europe and you see that it is true. Except Europe is cuter than here.

Most places in Europe are famous for the food, athough with the euro and the dollar, who knows what you can actually afford.

LITTLE TRICK

Everyone in Europe speaks English, but don't be lazy. Learn a little of the language of everywhere you go—a little French, a little Italian, a little Spanish. Then, when you're there, speak the language, and it will feel as though you are visiting entirely different countries!

Do This

Travel! See the world!

It is broadening and you can't believe how quaint other places are.

PASSPORT

United States of America

Take pictures with people in them.

Not That!

Take chances in horrible places.

India, Africa, and Asia: forget it. Japan *maybe*.

HIDDEN DANGER

Remember Hitler and the Nazis got their start in Europe, so don't kid yourself. There is still a lot of anti-Semitism, so stick to the museums.

Look for trouble in South America.

It has nothing to do with do-you-believe-in-God. I know you don't believe in God and most of the time I don't, either. All you have to do is take one look at the people who really *do* believe in God— the *frummies*, the evangelical *goyim*, the poor uneducated people—and you get the message.

Still, it won't kill you to go through the motions. You meet your fellow Jews and say hello, isn't this nice, we're all Jews. And it reminds your children that they're Jewish. Is that so terrible?

Do This

Join a *shul* for Rosh Hashanah and Yom Kippur and make a nice seder for Passo

Who cares if it's boring. It's your heritage.

Go on Shabbos to meet the community.

Not That!

Go to *shul* three times a day.

No need to overdo it.

Hire someone to turn the lights on for you every Saturday.

0

Number of Jewish holidays from this list that I know what the holiday is all about:

- Tu B'Shvat
- Tishah b'Ab
- Lag B'Omer
- Simchas Torah
- Shemini Atzereth

PLEASURE? GUILTY!

What kind of person lives according to a book written five thousand years ago? What did they know about anything five thousand years ago? They thought the Earth was flat! We're supposed to listen to their rules about life?

So You Know

Evelyn's grandson, Jared or Jetson, something like that, is ten. *Can't wait.* Same thing with the girls. Diane Rosenberg's oldest daughter, the one who married what's-his-name, the CPA with the lawsuit and they got divorced— her girl had a lovely bat mitzvah. So apparently being bar mitzvahed is the "in" thing.

Do This

Make a bar mitzvah for the boys and a bat mitzvah for the girls.

> Evelyn Goldner from canasta says her grandson can't wait to be bar mitzvahed.

Celebrate your child *and* yourself.

46

Not That!

Go overboard and hire a marching band or the Rolling Stones for the party.

Oy Vey!

Don't turn into one of those *me-shugganehs* who rent stadiums or a cruise ship. It's disgusting!

LITTLE TRICK

Send an invitation to your child's hero—a baseball player or writer or musician or actress to attend the party. But not that Madonna. Anyway, whoever. They won't come, but they'll probably send back a nice autographed note and a photo you can frame as a memento of the occasion. Or maybe even a check.

It's not nice and very vulgar.

Mess around with "confirmation," which is supposed to be for the *goyim*.

It's a way of saying to the world, "Jews live here," and what's wrong with that? Who cares what's inside? Some prayers or the Shema or something. You don't have to kiss it or bow down to it when you go into the house. It's just there as a symbol.

And don't tell me you can't because you're renting so you can't hammer things into the door. You can put up a mezuzah with anything. They probably have magnetic mezuzahs you can stick on a metal door frame, for all I know.

Do This

Put a mezuzah on the door frame.

Even if you live in an apartment.

Have a nice set of Shabbos candlesticks. Because why not?

Not That!

Display a wreath or a "Chanukah bush"!

Christmas doesn't get enough publicity, you have to help?

Put candy canes on your lawn.

49

Israel is the one place where, if you go there, and you are Jewish, they have to take you in. This is a wonderful thing. No one in the *entire world* is Jewish, except for the Jewish people, this small minority. And everybody points the finger. The Christians think we killed Christ. The Moslems hate us because we hate the Arabs because the Arabs hate us. Believe me, Nazis-schmatzis, there will always be anti-Semitism.

So you have to go. And you must take the children, although of course first you have to have them.

Do This

Visit Israel. Take the kids.

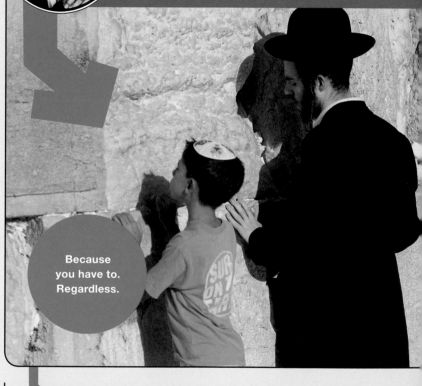

Because you have to. Regardless.

See the Wailing Wall in Jerusalem. Same reason.

Not That!

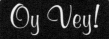

Move there.

You want to live in the desert? Try Palm Springs.

Spend a year on a *kibbutz*.

Oy Vey!

Even *without* the bombing. You've got umpteen political parties, and everyone is screaming at everyone else, constantly. Well, you know how Israelis are. So now imagine an entire *country* of Israelis. Which is what Israel is, after all.

15

◇◇◇◇◇◇◇

Number of people yelling their opinions at the same time when there are fifteen people in the room.

Once you are married and have children, it is easy to be tired. You go to work, you come home, you deal with the kids, you eat dinner. Then on the weekend you have the chores and the kids and the shopping and the do-it-yourself. The whole thing is very depleting.

Still, you have to see your male friends. It is very important for a man to be a man with other men. Otherwise you look up and it's ten years later and you get into trouble with the seven-year itch. You resent your wife and there's *tsurris*.

Do This

Play poker, where you can see your buddies and talk about what men talk about

It is important to have a peer group.

Have friends, even if they're not Jewish.

Not That!

...aste money on some psychiatrist who will ...l you to blame everything on your mother.

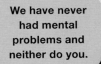

We have never had mental problems and neither do you.

Do Scientology, like what's-his-name, the actor.

Oy Vey!

All this talking about yourself to some stranger—it never stops! Look at Woody Allen. Seeing a psychiatrist for what— fifty years? It's a vicious cycle! It makes you crazy so you keep going.

It's fine to have a career, but they're your children and they need their mother. So for several years you're home with them, talking baby-talk and changing diapers twenty-four hours a day.

That's why you should learn these group games, so you can have adult interactions and maybe enjoy a glass of wine. Get a sitter for a few hours or have your husband watch the kids on the weekend. Or maybe you'll have a nanny or an au pair or whatever, although God knows I didn't.

Do This

Learn canasta or mah-jongg so you can get together with your girlfriends.

It is important to take a break and dish the dirt.

Try bridge, too, although I never played it.

Not That!

Waste money on a therapist so you can blame everything on me.

It's easy to complain when you don't know the pressures I was under.

Start drinking or taking tranquilizers in secret.

Oy Vey!

You think you have problems now? Wait until you have children. You do all the right things, and then they grow up and want to pay some stranger to tell them how terrible you were.

You would think, with modern science, that people would be less allergic to everything, but it seems to be the opposite. Janice Polan's granddaughter ate some cookie made with peanuts and practically dropped dead. The doctor was Sherman Himmelfarb, we met his parents on that cruise to Saint Martin last year. It's half French and half Dutch. French, fine, but who eats Dutch?

Your tonsils used to swell up in the summer. These days they make you keep your tonsils. Tonsils, appendix, adenoids—all those things we used to throw away.

Do This

Have a dog or a cat, as long as no one is allergic.

First get everyone tested at the dermatologist. For everything. Just in case.

Fish are easy if you just get one.

Not That!

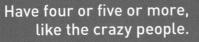

Have four or five or more, like the crazy people.

If they want to live on a farm, they should live on a farm.

Or turtles and hamsters, which are unsanitary.

If There Is One Thing I Know

Believe me, you never know what can happen. You go out to dinner, somebody trips and falls, and suddenly everyone is suing everybody else. You think, "I don't behave that way. I don't make a legal to-do about every little thing." It doesn't matter. *They do.* They send their lawyer after *you,* so you have to have one to send after *them.*

Meanwhile, of course, in the end no one ends up with anything except the lawyers. This is our society. It's terrible but it's the world we live in.

Do This

Get a good lawyer and a good accountant.

Because you never know. Especially in this day and age.

Find an insurance agent you don't mistrust.

Not That!

Waste your time with hypnotherapists, astrologers, psychics, or those types.

If this stuff really worked, science would know. Forget it.

Bother with stock brokers. Those *goniffs*.

Men age more acceptably than women. Men look mature. Women look old. It's not fair but what else is new? So women are entitled to have a little procedure every now and then. Which, by the way, becomes even more important now that everyone gets divorced at the drop of a hat. Because then you're back on the market and in competition with all the younger girls.

Look, I'm done. Your father and I will be together until we drop dead. But if I were thirty years younger I would think about it.

Do This

Have "some work" done when the time comes.

It's not a question of vanity. It's a question of self-respect.

Have fun with your hair. That's okay.

Not That!

Embarrass yourself by trying to look thirty-nine forever.

Whatever you see in the mirror is not what everyone else sees.

PLEASURE? GUILTY!

It's better to look a little younger than old, but it's better to look old than like someone who's trying too hard to look a lot younger. Unless that's all you care about, and you want to attract . . . you know . . . *shmegegis*.

HIDDEN DANGER

And don't do anything to your lips. You've seen those pictures. These women, they look like their lips were stuffed with cotton and closed up on a sewing machine. By a person who makes scarecrows!

Futz and *fumfer* with your hair excessively.

61

You Must Already Know

They wear anything these days. You get on a plane, there are men in sleeveless undershirts and sandals. You go to a Broadway show, everyone is wearing rags and sneakers.

Going out should be different than staying home. You go to Rome, the Italians walk around, everyone is beautifully dressed. It makes a person feel good! You feel, I am partaking of a civilization of intelligent people!

So wear a skirt, a dress, some nice pants when you go out. Just remember to take a sweater. Because why not?

Do This

Wear some nice pants and a sweater when you go out.

Or a skirt and a sweater.

Don't let your husband wear jeans. We're not farmers.

Not That!

...out in public in a hooker's skirt or whatever the kids are wearing these days.

It's not sexy. It's cheap. There's a difference. At least there used to be.

Wear *drek* just to be "comfortable."

Oy Vey!

Will you please tell me something? At night, when people go out, why does everyone dress either like a prostitute or a beatnik? Like either a sexpot or a slob? Is this the world we now live in?

HIDDEN DANGER

These tight, sexy garments—you could end up attracting a bad element. They think you're teasing them and they won't take no for an answer. That's all I need.

Mother Decoder ∞∞∞∞∞∞∞∞∞∞∞∞∞∞

At a Restaurant
"Let me ask you something. Do the children know they're Jewish?"

WHAT IT MEANS: "I know you're very modern, with your lack of religious belief and everything, but are you making at least a token effort to respect the five thousand years of tradition your father and I made an effort to present to you? Or were we wrong about that, too?"

When Visiting
"I love the way you live." (Pause) "It's not how I would choose to live, but. . . ."

WHAT IT MEANS: "The battle to educate and refine you into becoming an acceptably sophisticated, presentable human being has long been lost. All I can do now is be polite."

On the Phone
"And how is your wife?"

WHAT IT MEANS: "I don't actually like the woman you married, but we both know how heedless and naïve you can be, so it's out of my hands. To pretend to be loving and attentive I'll ask about her, but not to the point where I will condescend to actually mention her name."

At Your Sibling's Seder

"You don't know how much work this is. Didn't she do a wonderful job?"

WHAT IT MEANS: "Whether 'she' refers to your sister, or to your brother's wife, the point is, she did everything—all the cooking, cleaning, decorating, and arranging—single-handedly. Like I used to. (And even if she didn't—since she also works full-time—I will pretend that she did.) And like you or your wife should do next Passover, if you can make an effort to be a little less selfish and above-it-all."

At Your Child's Bar Mitzvah

"I had no idea this kind of casual dress was 'in.' "

WHAT IT MEANS: "Reform is one thing. But can't your friends respect those of us who think a suit and tie should be worn to *shul*?"

Holidays and Special Occasions

◇◇◇◇◇◇◇◇◇◇◇◇◇◇◇◇◇◇

Many People Don't Know

You're welcoming the baby boy into the Jewish family by cutting off his foreskin. I suppose it's rather primitive. But the Jews are an old ancient people! And it's *symbolic*. It's not voodoo, like with the Catholics and the wafer and the wine and all that body and blood *meshugas*.

At least it's perfectly safe. The *mohel* has done this a thousand times. If it's your son's, just make sure your wife doesn't pass out. If it's someone else's, who cares—the whole thing takes a minute and then you have a party.

Do This

Just smile.

Of course it's strange. Accept it.

Say, "It's an interesting ritual, isn't it?"

Not That!

Make jokes, like "That has to hurt!" or any of your smart remarks.

Don't encourage the non-Jews to make fun.

Make comical faces of pain.

PLEASURE? GUILTY!

Any non-Jews in the audience are going to either be a little upset by the ceremony or snide and snickery about how "the Jews" are. So don't make jokes. It won't kill you for once to just show some respect.

Oy Vey!

Some smart aleck on the radio said that circumcision is "genital mutilation." Absolute nonsense. And if someone at the ceremony says that, you can tell them to go to hell.

You Know Very Well

It goes without saying that if you're leading the seder you have to preside and make sure it moves along. But even if you're just one of the group, it is ill-mannered to get *schnockered* while everyone around you is trying to make a nice service.

Let alone it sets a bad example for the children. Not that they're going to get *potschkied* then and there, God forbid. Although who knows, these days, with what you hear about the young people. But in terms of attitude.

Do This

Take a few sips for each of the four "cups" of wine.

Set an example for the children.

Add water to your glass.

Not That!

Guzzle an entire glass every time, because "the Haggadah told me to."

PLEASURE? GUILTY!

I know it can be boring, and your father is losing his sight so he can't read as fast. And the book is ordering you to drink. But it says "cups." Not "glasses" or "wine glasses" or "fancy French balloon goblets like goldfish bowls on a stem." So take it easy.

Especially if there are non-Jewish guests present.

Oy Vey!

I'm not saying, don't make *any* jokes. Remember your Uncle Mel, when we had the seders at his house? So serious and depressing you wanted to slit your wrists.

Get *farshnoshket* because "it's a celebration."

I Don't Know If You Knew

Chanukah is more an American holiday. They barely observe it in Israel. And forget eight days of giving presents. Strictly American. Well, it's obvious why. To compete with Christmas. Not "compete," but to compensate. So Jewish children don't feel left out of all the gift-giving and present-receiving.

I don't know the rules for *dreidel*. You can look them up. It's a betting game. You put coins or whatever in the *pushke* and then spin and whatever it turns up is whether you win, lose, or draw.

Do This

Play *dreidel* with the kids.

Chanukah is for the children.

Help make *latkes* or even those deep-fried doughnuts.

Not That!

Get drunk.

I know it's supposedly a "party" but like I said, it's for the children. Of course there will be drinks and alcohol, but please. It's a family event. And anyway, who can do a lot of drinking and flirting with all those children running around?

HIDDEN DANGER

You have candles, which get all melty and drippy. And you have *latkes*, which are fried in oil. And you have children eating chocolate *gelt*. So what it means is there is ample opportunity to get terrible stains on your clothes.

This isn't the office, and it's not a Christmas party.

Make time with women whether you're married or not.

Do This

As Everyone
Including
You Knows

Most women are
neither ugly nor
beautiful, but
ordinary-looking,
and they end up
looking very nice
once they're all done
up for their wedding
day. But sometimes
you do get a girl who
really is not very
attractive. And so
at her wedding she
looks like a not-very-
attractive girl in a
wedding dress.

This can be a
little sad, because
everyone is try-
ing so hard to be
hypnotized with the
bride's beauty. But
just *shvaig*. Don't say
anything. Even in
private. Let her have
her day.

Tell the bride she looks beautiful.

Even if she's
a *meeskite* in
a gown.

Tell *others* she looks beautiful.

Not That!

Get cute in the reception line and say, "You look so different!"

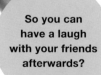

So you can have a laugh with your friends afterwards?

Tell people you're with, "It's downhill from here."

PLEASURE? GUILTY!

They say men are competitive in sports and business, but women are competitive with each other. Socially. It's human nature. Well, if your friends at the wedding get catty and bitchy, just walk away. Maybe your friends are jealous. Did you ever think of that?

Oy Vey!

I just realized I don't know what to tell you about gay people getting married. I'm all for it, because love is love, and look at the *meshuganehs* who are against it. But I have no idea what the rules are at the wedding!

You Can't Not Know

Your father and I have the same fight every Yom Kippur. He thinks I'm too cheerful and I think he's fooling himself about atoning. He thinks that if he pretends hard enough it will be true. That's what all religion is, if you ask me.

Anyway, the Yom Kippur service is to be part of the community, and maybe for a minute think about how to be a better person in the next year. I do that, and I seriously doubt that I ever actually improve. So I try to be agreeable.

Do This

Be pleasant.

Why not? Because you're "atoning"?

Act accepting. You're not God.

Not That!

Look put-upon, depressed, or guilty.

LITTLE TRICK

If you really do feel bad about something, what will help is talking to an actual person. Not me, of course, since I'm your mother and God forbid I should know anything. But talk to the rabbi. I'm serious. It doesn't matter if he's "wise." He'll be objective and you'll get it off your chest. That's his job.

There are more effective ways to atone for something than by asking God.

HIDDEN DANGER

Between fasting and the long service, you could pass out. Does God want Jews to faint? I seriously doubt it. He wants Jews to be healthy. So before you fast eat a big breakfast.

Encourage everyone else to be depressed, too.

Take This, Not That! ◇◇◇◇◇◇◇◇◇◇

Drinking

TAKE THIS: Drink Chivas or J&B or Dewar's.
NOT THAT: Smoke marijuana or that crack.

TAKE THIS: Drink a couple of beers while watching the game.
NOT THAT: Drink a couple of cases of beer until you can't even see the TV.

TAKE THIS: Have a nice bottle of wine with dinner.
NOT THAT: Drink three vodka martinis and then have a bottle of wine with dinner.

Drugs

TAKE THIS: Go to a show or a movie to cheer up.
NOT THAT: Take antidepressants for the rest of your life.

TAKE THIS: Maybe take a Valium once and a while. In an emergency.
NOT THAT: Get addicted to Percodan or Oxy-whatsis or other hard drugs.

TAKE THIS: Have a cup of tea and read a book in bed to fall asleep.
NOT THAT: Take Ambien, which makes people crazy.

Do This, Not That— For the Children!

◇◇◇◇◇◇◇◇◇◇◇◇◇◇◇◇◇◇◇◇

Children don't care about "variety." They like to hear the same story ten thousand times and watch the same movie a hundred million times. So going to Disney World again is perfectly great as far as they're concerned.

Of course it's torture on you and your wife, but tough. Once they're grown you'll have plenty of opportunity to not go there for the rest of your life.

LITTLE TRICK

They're always constantly getting older, which means they have a different experience every time they go. So maybe you will, too, who knows.

Do This

Take them to Disney World. Again.

At that age you want them to have fun. Forget "exposed to new things."

Go to SeaWorld, with the dolphins.

Not That!

Take them fishing. Who fishes?

And on those boats! With the seasickness!

God forbid, go hunting. It's for the *goyim*.

Look, a lot of TV is *drek*, but a lot is nice and educational and acceptable. Plus they play those games. Not the killing games, but nice ones. And their friends have nice TVs too. Why should they feel deprived? If you're going to have a TV, then *have* one.

2

◇◇◇◇◇◇◇

Number of TVs we had when you were growing up. In our bedroom and in the basement. Now they have them in every room and in the kitchen *and* in the car!

Do This

Get a big-screen TV for the kids.

Because they watch it and play games and whatnot. It's important.

Get that whatchamacallit game. Where you move your arms.

Not That!

Make—or let—them take karate lessons like a hoodlum.

With the yelling and the hitting.

Let them take any martial arts. Martial means war!

By Now Even I Know

We used to have just plain camps. You played sports, you swam, you made ashtrays out of clay and necklaces out of plastic, you walked around the woods and whatever. Now everything is specialized. If a child wants to learn taxidermy there's probably a camp for it.

So let the children pick their camps. What, it's expensive? What isn't? We'll treat. And, Mister Smart Guy, if the kids are away for a couple weeks, that means you and your wife can have some R and R, too, hint hint.

Do This

Send them to the summer camp they want.

With the musicals for her and the computers for him.

Send them to the camp you went to!

Not That!

Make them go to the one where you have to sleep in tents and get poison ivy.

If it's so good to "rough it," you go.

Send them on one of those Outside Bound wilderness nightmares.

As I Know You Know

You went to Hebrew school three days a week for six years. And you loved it! Well, maybe you hated it. But it was part of your education and it got you ready for your Bar Mitzvah. You can still read Hebrew to this day, can't you?

It's part of their absorbing their identity as Jews. And maybe the teachers are better now. They're more up-to-date and "with it."

Although I don't know what that means. But the kids do. Anyway, just do it.

Do This

Make sure the children go to Hebrew school.

No, I never went. Because I never had the opportunity!

Move back here and send them to yours!

Not That!

Let them get a job because "they need money."

PLEASURE? GUILTY!

I understand how you want to give your children the opportunities you didn't have as a child. But what kind of "job" can these *pishers* get? That's more important than their education? What is this, 1911 and we all just got off the boat?

They'll have the whole rest of their lives to work.

HIDDEN DANGER

If you don't send them to Hebrew school, they may completely forget that they're Jewish. They won't be ready for their Bar Mitzvah, they won't know the history—they might as well be Christian!

Let them skip Hebrew school because you hated it.

I read about what college costs these days. It is unbelievable and a *shanda*. When you went to college it *cost*, it wasn't free, but still. Where does all that money go?

Anyway, it's important to send them to the best college they can get into. You meet a better variety of people there besides the learning and the erudite surroundings and all that. Especially if the kids are going to be doctors and lawyers.

Do This

Take out a second mortgage to pay for a private university.

It's outrageous. But what can you do?

Rob a bank. I'm kidding.

Not That!

Send her to the state school.

So that what— she can play football?

Send her to some performing arts "college."

Oy Vey!

The lower quality the college, the more she'll be surrounded by rowdy *putzes* who get drunk all the time and knock over statues. And the girls will be those stuck-up sorority princesses whose parents probably hate Jews. Does that sound like a suitable environment?

HIDDEN DANGER

And then, God forbid, what if she marries a fraternity *putz*? While you're saving money! I can't even think about it.

Glossary ◇◇◇◇◇◇◇◇◇◇◇◇

Bris The ceremony where the *mohel* cuts off the boy baby's foreskin. The baby cries, the mother faints, and everyone else has a party.

Dreidel A top the kids play a little gambling game with during Chanukah. Each side has a Hebrew letter which stands for something, don't ask me what. "Hurray for God" or whatever.

Drek You know—junk. Crap. Inferior merchandise. Let's just leave it at that.

Farkakte Lousy, stupid, et cetera. You want a for instance? "Why is your father depressed? Because the *farkakte* Orioles just lost a double-header."

Farschnoshket Exactly what it sounds like—drunk.

Fartik It means "the end," or "it's over," or "period." "Never mind you didn't like the waitress's attitude. Just leave her the tip and *fartik*, we're going home."

Feh Phooey. Yuck. An expression of not liking something.

Fressing Eating heartily. Actually, pigging out, if you must know.

Frum Pronounced, not "from," but like the "tum" in tumult. Orthodox, observant. So "the *frummies*" are the people who are *frum*, although it's not a real word.

Fumfer It really means a speaker's error, but I use it to mean the same thing as *futz*. Who knows why.

Futz Fool around, mess around. "Don't *futz* with it! Call the cable company."

Gelt German for "gold." Money.

Gevalt You know, I'm not sure what it literally means. Isn't that a riot? "Heaven forbid," maybe. "*Oy gevalt*" means "oh no," but with emphasis.

Goniff A thief, a swindler. "Her husband is a doll, yes, but his brother? Please. A complete *goniff*."

Gotteniu An anguished cry, meaning, "oh, God!"

Goyim/Goyishe Oh come on. Everybody knows this. *Goyim* is the plural of goy, which means, a Gentile. *Goyishe* means "*goy*-like," or non-Jewish as an adjective.

Hotzeplotz A made-up fantasy place, meaning, unreasonably far away. Like Timbuktu.

Keyna hore This literally means, "no Evil Eye." You say it to ward off bad luck after hearing good news ("She's pregnant, *keyna hore*.").

Kibbutz A collective farm in Israel.

Kvell To beam with pride and joy thanks to your children or their children.

Latkes Potato pancakes. Traditional for Chanukah because of the oil they're cooked in. Some magical oil burned for eight days when the Romans destroyed the Temple—look, never mind.

Meshuge/Meshugas Crazy. An adjective. *Meshugas* means craziness, but particular to someone. As in, "Esther Feldman just became president of the Sisterhood at the *shul*. So now we have to deal with her *meshugas*."

Mohel The man who performs a bris. Usually a rabbi. Cutting off thousands of foreskins—can you imagine? Well, at least he knows what he's doing.

Pisher A little child, an immature kid. "Do you know what they give that *pisher* for an allowance? Fifty dollars a week!"

Potschkied I'll tell you something—we use it to mean "drunk," but it doesn't really mean that. To "*potschky* around" means to waste time. So sue me.

Pushke The kitty in a card game. You ante up into the *pushke*.

Putz A jerk, a slob, a loser. Yes, even a Jew can be such a thing.

Schlep To carry or drag along in a laborious manner. Or to take an arduous trip when you don't really want to. "What, I'm supposed to *schlep* downtown just to find decent rye bread?"

Schlump A slob, perhaps also with a dimension of being lazy.

Schmuck A jerk, like *putz*.

Schnockered Drunk. Yes, there are several words for this. So what?

Shanda An appalling shame; a scandalous shame. "And the worst part? Monica Lewinsky was a Jewish girl. Such a *shanda*!"

Shmegegis Like *putz*, but plural. Losers, nudniks.

Shmendrik Like *shmegegis*. Another word for loser or jerk. (*Oy*.)

Sheygets A non-Jewish male. As you may know, *shiksa* is a non-Jewish girl.

Shul Synagogue. German for "school."

Tam "Soul," in that African-American way. Spark, zest, depth, and so on.

Tsedrayt Confused, nuts, disoriented. There's twenty words for this, too.

Tsurris Trouble, hot water.

Tumul Confusion, uproar.

Index ◇◇◇◇◇◇◇◇◇◇◇◇◇◇◇◇◇

A

Africa, condition of as being out of the question 43
Allergic, failure of modern science to make
　people less 56
"Artist," so-called 13

B

Baby, frightened by screaming 26; desire to
　pretend hasn't been born 27
Bar mitzvah, 65; anticipation by Evelyn Goldner's
　grandson of 46
Ballet, taking of 30
Beach, the 40, 41
Boy, Jewish, nice 16, 29
Bride, complimenting appearance of no
　matter what 74
Bris, possible opinion of modern person of 28
Brokers, stock, characterized 59

C

Camp, 86–87; site of your son taking off his bathing
　suit 29
Canasta, importance of 54
Cards, credit 21
Cat, a dog or a 56; mental condition of people
　who have four or five 57
"Chanukah bush," pretense of 49
Chickens, treatment of 37
Children, have 4; ideal quantity of 5; how you
　will raise 17
Christ, Jesus, non-belief in 17
Christmas, spurious need of publicity of 49
Circumcising, 5,000-year problem-free
　history of 28
Cities, behavior of people who live in 24
College, the importance of a good 10
Computer, injunction against starting with 4

Country club, 38; site of your son taking off his
　bathing suit 29
"Creative," something so-called, advice against doing 4

D

Dancing, tap, characterized 31
Diets, a million 36
Doctor(s), a, perennial employment of 18;
　as good providers 18; advice from a Jewish
　mother to marry acknowledged as amusing 18
Donna, my cousin 59

E

Europe, relative cuteness of compared to here 42

F

Father, your 14, 32, 40
Fishing, inadvisability of taking children 83
Foreskin, not having a 29
Friends, your male 52
Frummies, large families of characterized 5

G

Goldner, Evelyn 46
Golf course, half of world's business conducted on 38
Goyim 25, 33, 44, 47, 49

H

Harriet, lovely daughter of 14
Health, your children's, your husband's, yours 5
Himmelfarb, Sherman, parents of whom we met on
　that cruise 56
Homemaker, a good 20
Hoodlum(s), and bad posture 8; and karate lessons
　85; and jumping in waves 41
Horowitz, Lil 5
Hotzeplotz 5
Hypnotherapists, astrologers, psychics, etc. 59

I

Israel 50, population consists almost entirely
of Israelis 51
Italians, effect of beautiful dressing 62

J

JDate, means by which Lil Horowitz's daughter met
that Jeffrey 5

K

Kippur, Yom, irrelevance of its being boring 44, 76
Kosher, as being up to you 37

L

Lawyer(s) 12, 19, necessity of sending yours after them
once they send theirs after you 58
Lessons, piano 30

M

Mah-jongg, as valuable context of adult interactions 54
Married, get, contrasted with stalling 4, 5
Mezuzah, genuflection to not required 48
Models, fashion, necessity to look like questioned 34

N

Nathan, your cousin 15

O

"Off, taking a year" 11

P

Party, Chanukah, inappropriateness of flirting at 73
Patinkin, Mandy, posture of 8
Penis(es) 29
People, Jewish, the, as being only Jews in the world 50
People, stupid, abundance of in the United States 25
Polan, Janice 56
Problems, mental, frequency of our having 53
Psychiatrists, all they tell you 53

R

Roll, rock and, ploy to prevent children learning 31
Rose, Aunt 8
Rosenberg, Diane 46
Rosh Hashanah, join a *shul* for 44
Russia, apparent falling-apart of 43

S

Scandinavia, safeness of acknowledged 43
School, Hebrew, hatred of by you 88
Seder, 70; your selfishness demonstrated by not
hosting a 65
Sex life, normal standards for your 32, 33
Sheba, Queen of, vanity of criticized 5, 21
Shul, ordering attendance of 44
Sky-diving, mindset of practitioner of 39
Slob, dressing like a 63
Saint Martin, dual nature of 56
Stones, The Rolling, reasons for not hiring 47
Sweater, wear a 38, remember to take a 62

T

Tam, defined as meaning "*tam*" 24
Teacher, a, reality of 13; problems of 13; as husband 18
Therapist, wasting money on 55

U

University, private, cost of 90
University, state, curriculum of 91

V

Vegan, as state of being *tsedrayt* 37

W

Wedding, a lovely 22; who for 22; ploy of skipping 23
Wife, your, state of my not actually liking 64
"Work, some," having done 60
World, the, see 42

Image Credits ◇◇◇◇◇◇◇◇◇◇◇◇◇◇◇◇◇◇◇◇◇◇◇◇◇◇◇◇◇◇◇◇◇◇

becker&mayer! extends special thanks to model Carolyn Cox, stylist Dawn Tunnell, and TCM Models and Talent. Also, a big thank you to J. Nichole Smith at dane + dane studios (www.dane-dane.com) for supplying the original photography of our "mother" model throughout the book.

Every effort has been made to trace copyright holders. If any unintentional omissions have been made, becker&mayer! would be pleased to add appropriate acknowledgments in future editions.

Page 8: © iStockphoto.com/4x6
Page 9: © iStockphoto.com/izusek
Page 10: © iStockphoto.com/junial
Page 11: © iStockphoto.com/sdominick
Page 12: © iStockphoto.com/serg3d
Page 13: © iStockphoto.com/jgroup
Page 14: © Thinkstock, LLC
Page 15: © iStockphoto.com/dolgikh
Page 16: © Peter Dazeley
Page 17: © iStockphoto.com/Alija
Page 18: © iStockphoto.com/geotrac
Page 19: © iStockphoto.com/morganl
Page 20: © Tim Bieber
Page 21: © iStockphoto.com/iconogenic
Page 22: © Buccina Studios
Page 23: © Christoph Wilhelm
Page 24: © iStockphoto.com/Lingbeek
Page 25: © iStockphoto.com/lisegagne
Page 26: © Jupiterimages
Page 27: © iStockphoto.com/LeifStiller
Page 28: © iStockphoto.com/stuartpitkin
Page 29: © iStockphoto.com/Angel_1978
Page 30: © iStockphoto.com/leezsnow
Page 31: © Siri Stafford
Page 32: © iStockphoto.com/1001nights
Page 33: © Jeffrey Hamilton
Page 34: © iStockphoto.com/sjlocke
Page 35: © iStockphoto.com/lisegagne
Page 36: © iStockphoto.com/JoeGough
Page 37: © iStockphoto.com/diego_cervo
Page 38: © iStockphoto.com/ginosphotos
Page 39: © Terje Rakke
Page 40: © iStockphoto.com/YinYang
Page 41: © Peter Dazeley
Page 42: © iStockphoto.com/DNY59
Page 43: © iStockphoto.com/HenriFaure
Page 44: © iStockphoto.com/pushlama
Page 45: © Rob Melnychuk

Page 46: © iStockphoto.com/edelmar
Page 47: © Ryan McVay
Page 48: © iStockphoto.com/Terryfic3D
Page 49: © iStockphoto.com/DNY59
Page 50: © Gil Azouri
Page 51: © iStockphoto.com/amite
Page 52: © iStockphoto.com/stray_cat
Page 53: © iStockphoto.com/JeanellNorvell
Page 54: © Brand X Pictures
Page 55: © iStockphoto.com/syagci
Page 56: © iStockphoto.com/MoniqueRodriguez
Page 57: © iStockphoto.com/GlobalP
Page 58: © iStockphoto.com/lisafx
Page 59: © iStockphoto.com/CREATISTA
Page 60: © iStockphoto.com/jibilein
Page 61: © Troy Aossey
Page 62: © iStockphoto.com/sjlocke
Page 63: © iStockphoto.com/Laser222
Page 68: © iStockphoto.com/izusek
Page 69: © iStockphoto.com/joshblake
Page 70: © iStockphoto.com/tovfla
Page 71: © iStockphoto.com/Blue_Cutler
Page 72: © iStockphoto.com/JBryson
Page 73: © iStockphoto.com/EricHood
Page 74: © iStockphoto.com/TriggerPhoto
Page 75: © iStockphoto.com/IZI1947
Page 76: © iStockphoto.com/hidesy
Page 77: © Donna Day
Page 82: © Dario Mitidieri
Page 83: © iStockphoto.com/MidwestWilderness
Page 84: © iStockphoto.com/sjlocke
Page 85: © iStockphoto.com/PhotoEuphoria
Page 86: © iStockphoto.com/nataq
Page 87: © Dennis Hallinan
Page 88: © iStockphoto.com/hsandler
Page 89: © White Packert
Page 90: © iStockphoto.com/SchulteProductions
Page 91: © iStockphoto.com/arsenik